WHO DO YOU THINK YOU ARE, CHARLIE BROWN?

CHARLES M. SCHULZ

Selected Cartoons from
PEANUTS EVERY SUNDAY Vol. 1

A Fawcett Crest Book

FAWCETT PUBLICATIONS, INC., GREENWICH, CONN.
MEMBER OF AMERICAN BOOK PUBLISHERS COUNCIL, INC.

WHO DO YOU THINK YOU ARE, CHARLIE BROWN

This book, prepared especially for Fawcett Publications, Inc.
comprises the first half of PEANUTS EVERY SUNDAY, and is
published by arrangement with Holt, Rinehart and Winston, Inc.

First Fawcett Crest Printing, February 1968

Published by Fawcett World Library
67 West 44th Street, New York, N.Y.
Printed in the United States of America.

CLOMP

WHEW!

ARE YOU CRAZY? IT'S **COLD** OUTSIDE! YOU COULD CATCH PNEUMONIA ROLLING AROUND OUT THERE IN THE SNOW!

THE STRUGGLE FOR SECURITY KNOWS NO SEASON!

IN OTHER WORDS YOU CAN'T FIGHT CITY HALL!

THAT'S RIGHT!

NOW, GO ON HOME, AND FORGET THE WHOLE THING..

WHEW I WAS SCARED TO DEATH SOMEONE WASN'T GOING TO COME ALONG AND TALK ME OUT OF IT!